THE
ENNEAGRAM
TYPE 9
journal

A Guide to Inner Work & Self-Discovery

for The Peacemaker

THIS JOURNAL BELONGS TO:

Published in the United States by: Hay House LLC: www.hayhouse.com®
Published in Australia by: Hay House Australia Publishing Pty Ltd: www.hayhouse.com.au
Published in the United Kingdom by: Hay House UK Ltd: www.hayhouse.co.uk
Published in India by: Hay House Publishers (India) Pvt Ltd: www.hayhouse.co.in

Cover design: Julie Davison
Interior design: Lisi Mohandessi
Author photo: Courtesy of Deborah Threadgill Egerton, Ph.D.

Tradepaper ISBN: 978-1-4019-7909-6
10 9 8 7 6 5 4 3 2 1
1st edition, May 2024

This product uses responsibly sourced papers and/or recycled materials. For more information, see www.hayhouse.com.

Printed and bound by CPI Group (UK) Ltd, Croydon, CR0 4YY

MIX
Paper | Supporting
responsible forestry
FSC® C013604

THE
ENNEAGRAM
TYPE 9
journal

DEBORAH THREADGILL EGERTON, Ph.D.
& LISI MOHANDESSI

HAY HOUSE LLC
Carlsbad, California • New York City
London • Sydney • New Delhi

This journal is dedicated to
the many Walters in my life:
Father, Brother, Husband, & Son.
When I look at the pages of
my story, you continue to be the ink
that transforms the ordinary into
the reality of extraordinary love.

You are gifted with a body that allows you to be here in the present moment, a mind that opens access to unlimited possibilities to be explored, and a heart that holds the enormous capacity to love and be loved.

This is the authentic you. You will find yourself when you accept the beauty of your true nature.

Gratitude for who you are is the first step.

Grace will follow.

Caritas,
Deborah & Lisi

CONTENTS

*Enjoy your journey, and
may you find love and
light within yourself.*

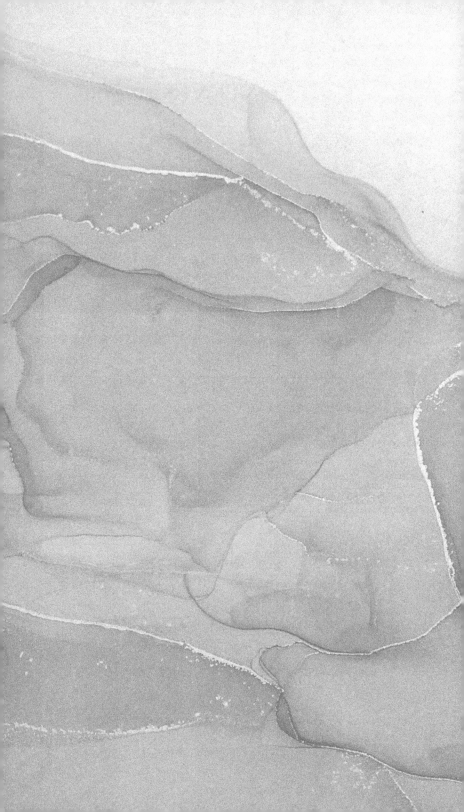

INTRODUCTION

Many of us journey through life pondering the reasons behind our actions and how we can enrich our lives. We seek not only improvement but also a sense of tranquility, productivity, and purpose. Conversations with friends, colleagues, mentors, and partners often echo the advice to "do the work." This phrase never fails to elicit a knowing smile because if it were that simple, we would already be immersed in the process of "doing the work." Yet we continually find ourselves returning to the fundamental question: What is the work?

A deep understanding of oneself is necessary to live a life brimming with abundance, creativity, joy, and love. Self-awareness is a journey inward, a voyage to explore how we present ourselves to the world, and the Enneagram will serve as our guide. Clues about our true selves are sometimes scattered before us, but we often choose to look away from anything that challenges our self-image. This is why the voyage inward, toward self-realization, becomes indispensable in uncovering our genuine, authentic selves.

This journal is thoughtfully crafted to accompany you on this very journey as you harness the insights of the Enneagram. Within these pages you'll encounter an array of writing prompts, mindfulness exercises, inspirational quotes, and grounding meditations for introspection. Each page is a deliberate step along your unique path. It's crucial to remember that this process cannot be hurried or coerced. Guidance on this voyage comes from a source known by many names—God, the Universe, the Divine, Spirit, or a name entirely personal to your experience. All these concepts are interconnected. You need not adhere to any dogmatic religious structure; what truly matters is connecting with that part of you that acknowledges a higher force, shaping and influencing your choices and your path forward.

This journal isn't something you casually dip into; rather, it's an invitation to cultivate a consistent habit of exploring its pages, allowing you to fully embrace the practices within. These pages are designed to guide you toward a profound understanding of why you do what you do.

The Enneagram stands out as a radiant gem among the many personality typing systems, and it beckons with a warm, unique approach centered on uncovering motivations rather than mere behaviors. It opens a doorway to explore the why behind our actions, inviting us to discover the roots of our behaviors. As we delve into this exploration, we find newfound flexibility, unlocking exciting possibilities we may have never imagined before.

We encourage you to delve deeper into the understanding of your dominant Enneagram energy, which is akin to picking up a mirror to gaze upon yourself in a way you've never done before. The idea may initially seem a bit intimidating, but the richness of your life is directly linked to the depth you're willing to explore within your soul.

Your life inherently possesses meaning, purpose, and a trajectory leading toward goodness; it's our natural inclination. Sometimes, we find ourselves needing to reconnect with what truly matters. We might start to wonder and feel disoriented when we sense that we've drifted away from our guiding light. But remember, that guidance hasn't abandoned us; it's possible we've simply strayed from it, unable to see what's right in front of us.

As you embark on this journey, we wish you all the goodness and benefits it has to offer. It's not about reaching a final destination but about following your guiding light, aligning yourself with what's genuine, trustworthy, and good in both the world and within yourself. Return to the pages of this journal daily, allowing your journey to inform you and lead you toward truth, joy, love, light, and goodness. All these elements reside within you, and they'll never abandon you. Sources of love and joy perpetually surround us, and by embracing the truth of goodness in the world, you'll radiate with the light found inside yourself.

This journal is designed as your reference guide and exploratory workbook. The following section will gently guide you through the Enneagram system and provide an overview of Type Nine energy. Within these pages, you'll find a wealth of knowledge about the Enneagram; and using this journal is a chance to reignite your inner connection with your Enneagram Nine energy. Prepare yourself, for your mind will be engaged, your heart will be touched, and your body will respond; all of these experiences, both uplifting and challenging, are an integral part of the journey. We hope you continue to revisit these pages as you further your journey deeper into the Enneagram system.

The Enneagram

The Enneagram is an archetypal personality system that combines modern psychological practices with a deep foundation in ancient traditions, religions, cultures, and spiritual practices. It is a model of the human psyche taught as a typology of nine personality archetypes. These types have names that reflect the nine different energies: Eight, Challenger; Nine, Peacemaker; One, Idealist; Two, Helper; Three, Achiever; Four, Individualist; Five, Investigator; Six, Loyalist; and Seven, Enthusiast.

The Enneagram invites you to embark on a journey of self-discovery, unlocking the intricate mechanisms governing your existence. It allows you to delve into the why behind your actions and the how of your daily functioning in pursuit of fulfilling your needs. Unveiling your core motivations, values, fears, and inherent strengths is a perpetual source of insight. Simultaneously, the Enneagram casts light on the egoic patterns that occasionally hinder our progress, thwarting our alignment with our true selves. More significantly, while this insightful system aids us in uncovering our authentic selves, it equally guides us in connecting with others, fostering appreciation, and cultivating genuine presence.

This beginning section is designed to serve as a refresher on the basics of the Enneagram and a quick look into each of the nine types. Remember: the Enneagram is a fluid system that provides access to all nine types, and we encourage you to explore your relationship with all of these energies.

The moment you intentionally chose to use this journal, you began your journey to discover who you really are instead of creating another version of yourself. Or, as people like to say, "the best version of yourself." Your goal now is to find out who you are underneath all the versions of yourself that you have created. Welcome to the journey of your lifetime! May you find joy, peace, acceptance, and belonging in this exploration. May love be your path, and may light shine on every step you take. Most importantly, may you fall deeply in love with the authentic you. The glorious being that you were created to be.

A QUICK OVERVIEW OF THE BASICS OF THE ENNEAGRAM

TYPE/POINT

Each of the nine Enneagram points possesses unique energies and characteristics. When discussing an Enneagram type, we are identifying the specific point on the Enneagram where one embodies the most significant energy. It's important to note that we have access to all nine points on the Enneagram, each contributing to our holistic understanding and personal growth.

CENTERS OF INTELLIGENCE

The Enneagram is explored through three Centers of Intelligence: Body, Heart, and Head. Sometimes, these centers, or triads, are called Body/Instinctive, Heart/Feeling, and Head/Thinking. Each center has a connection to particular emotions: the Body, anger and rage (Eight, Nine, One); the Heart, shame and guilt (Two, Three, Four); and the Head, fear and anxiety (Five, Six, Seven).

BASIC DESIRE AND BASIC FEAR

We all have inner drive and internalized fear that affect all of our behaviors, beliefs, and actions. You may resonate with all nine basic fears and desires, as we are beings composed of all nine energies; however, you will have the most substantial connection to one corresponding fear and desire of one specific type.

CORE MOTIVATION

The core motivation constantly challenges us to get what we most desire at any given moment while avoiding what we fear that will cause our demise. The core motivation is your internal drive, the reason you wake up in the morning, how you navigate life, and that thing that gets you going or paralyzes you. Think of the core motivation as why you do what you do.

WINGS

The types on either side of your dominant Enneagram energy affect how your type shows up in the world. Every Enneagram type has two wings; however, one of the wings may significantly influence the energy of your dominant Enneagram type.

LINES AND ARROWS

The Enneagram lines and arrows, also referred to as the stress and security points or directions of growth and stress, connect the types across the map. There are multiple ways of using the lines and arrows when we see them as connections to pick up specific qualities at specific times. We can move freely between these connections, picking up positive and negative energies as we need them to create a warning system and a path for growth.

PASSION: THE WAY WE SUFFER—PERSONAL CHALLENGE

The passions represent the nine main ways we lose our center, become more susceptible to personality distortions, and become disoriented from reality. We can refer to each of the passions as the way in which each type suffers.

FIXATION: HOW WE GET STUCK—THE TRAP

We all have a way of becoming trapped in our personality, which we see play out through the fixation. These "traps" are mental blocks we hold on to when attempting to justify our reality.

VIRTUE: OUR TRUE NATURE—THE GIFT

Honoring our true selves and who we become develops when we land in our virtue. These specific characteristics manifest through the emotional awareness of the authentic self, and the letting go of ego, self-deception, and dynamic vices. When we access our virtue, we become selfless and altruistic in our actions, feelings, and beliefs.

INSTINCTS

The Instincts, sometimes referred to as Subtypes and Instinctual Variants, within each Enneagram energy are Self-Preservation, Social, and Sexual (sometimes referred to as One-on-One). The Instincts can be mirrored in the three drives for survival: preserving life and focusing on physical needs, mutual cooperation and creating social bonds, and species survival through exploration and experiencing energies. We have a dominant instinct that we feel most comfortable with and a secondary instinct to support the dominant one. The third instinct is usually the least developed, therefore, an area that manifests as an unseen personal challenge.

LEVELS OF DEVELOPMENT

The Levels of Development established by Don Riso and Russ Hudson demonstrate the varying degrees of how each type can show up in the world based on presence. Healthy, average, and unhealthy refer to the Levels of Development and the overall state of a person's ability to function. The energy of each type can show up very differently depending on how healthy or unhealthy the individual is; this is a common reason why many people mistype or feel uncomfortable as their dominant type.

Healthy—Becoming expansive and unconstricted in essence, fully present in the world

Average—Beginning to allow our egos to guide our behaviors, dropping into destructive patterns when we fall asleep to our true selves, with a fluctuation of presence

Unhealthy—Dysfunctional and destructive behaviors when ego becomes the driving force behind everything we do; falling into ego-based patterns that trap us in personality

HEALTHY	L1	BEING	Freedom from Ego Structure
	L2	ALLOWING	Psychological Capacity ("I Am")
	L3	DOING	Social Value / Gift
AVERAGE	L4	EFFORTING	Social Role / Imbalance
	L5	IMPOSING	Interpersonal Control
	L6	AGGRESSION	Overcompensation
UNHEALTHY	L7	VIOLATING	Violation
	L8	COMPULSIVE	Delusion & Compulsion
	L9	DESTROYING	Pathological Destruction

ADAPTED FROM THE RISO-HUDSON LEVELS OF DEVELOPMENT

THINGS TO REMEMBER

- There are nine points on the Enneagram map. We can access all the points but lead with one dominant type. The numbers are not a scale, meaning no type is better or worse than any other type. However, in order to keep the Enneagram energies grouped by the centers of intelligence, we look at the types in this order: Eight, Nine, One, Two, Three, Four, Five, Six, Seven.

- Your dominant Enneagram type does not change throughout your life or shift based on your home or work life. You are born into your type and your experiences adjust how you navigate life, access your wing energy, travel with the arrows, and drop into the Levels of Development.

- No type is inherently gendered or dependent on dimensions of diversity (perceived race, socioeconomic status, education, age, religion, etc.). While the descriptions and energies of the types are universal and are not dependent on certain identifying factors, it is essential to note how an Enneagram energy can vary based on cultural or environmental influences or psychological well-being. For instance, some cultures have specific gender roles, socially acceptable values, or religious influences that can impact the Enneagram energy. Still, these factors do not fundamentally change a person's dominant Enneagram type.

- No one can tell you where you stand on the Enneagram map. You find your place by reading about and exploring all aspects of the nine types. Tests can help you narrow down the choices, and you may find your type by process of elimination. Tests are not always the defining factor of where you stand on the Enneagram map; the tests' quality matters.

KEY DESCRIPTORS OF THE NINE TYPES

The descriptors for each Enneagram type listed below begin on the high side of the energy and transition into the low side of the energy.

THE BODY CENTER

8 self-confident, authoritative, hardworking, strong-willed, forceful, passionate, outspoken, independent, protective, abundant energy, maintaining power and control, defensive, combative, "invulnerable," harsh, rageful, vengeful, boastful, demonstrative, tyrannical, omnipotent

9 receptive, reassuring, agreeable, considerate, quiet, easygoing, thoughtful, accepting, supportive, accommodating, dependable, stable, hardworking, pragmatic, complacent, disengaged, emotionally indolent, indifferent, angry, stubborn, dissociated, numb, apathetic

1 principled, purposeful, organized, ethical, fastidious, fair, objective, sense of mission, practical action, high standards, inner critic, highly critical, impatient, repressed, angry, controlling, perfectionistic, puritanical, resentful, emotionally constricted, scolding, abrasive, punitive, inflexible

THE HEART CENTER

2 generous, empathetic, helpful, thoughtful, caring, reliable, compassionate, kind, overly considerate, people-pleasing, seductive, intrusive, possessive, seeking validation, angry, resentful, hurt, manipulative, flattering, demonstrative, low self-esteem/value

3 hardworking, dedicated, driven, ambitious, resourceful, impressive, motivated, highly skilled, distinguished, pragmatic, opportunistic, calculating, narcissistic, impostor syndrome, seeking validation and attention, social climber, arrogant, unprincipled, self-centered, conceited

4 emotional, empathetic, creative, unique, connected, deep, romantic, authentic, eccentric, poetic, introspective, sensitive, moody, manipulative, judgmental, self-conscious, tormented, dark, depressive, angry, lost, self-destructive, hopeless, despair, macabre, self-absorbed

THE HEAD CENTER

5 competent, capable, cerebral, wise, highly skilled, well-rounded, eccentric, pioneering, complex, perceptive, independent, inventive, visionary, secretive, withdrawn, antagonistic, cynical, argumentative, reclusive, intellectually arrogant, self-destructive, nihilistic, erratic

6 innovative, structured, hardworking, intensely loyal, reliable, security-oriented, troubleshooting, revolutionary, engaging, contradictory, dependent, indecisive, untrusting, defensive, reactive, fearful, insecure, stubborn, suspicious, erratic, worst-case scenario, panicked, paranoid

7 free-spirited, fun, happy, curious, joyful, optimistic, adventurous, fast learners, well-rounded, humorous, bold, vivacious, life of the party, flaky, self-centered, narcissistic, emotionally stunted, insensitive, impulsive, escapist mentality, erratic, compulsive, panic-stricken, avoidance, jaded

**Which descriptors from your Enneagram energy
do you resonate with the most and why?**

_____

_____

_____

_____

_____

_____

_____

_____

_____

_____

_____

_____

Enneagram Type Nine

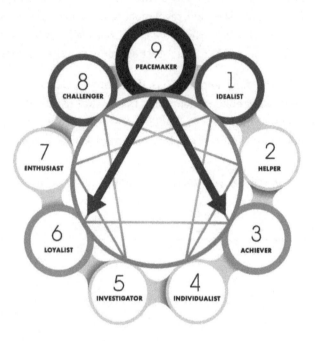

Descriptors for Nine Energy

easy-going, receptive, serene, harmonizing, reassuring, accepting, trusting, stable, mediator, calming, friendly, likable, positive thinking, loyal, self-effacing, indolent, frustrated, procrastination, "numb out," detached, self-forgetting, timid, avoidance tendencies, complacent, stubborn, passive-aggressive, self-abandoning, dissociated, neglectful

Basic Desire: to find inner peace, maintain stability, and preserve harmony

Basic Fear: to experience loss and separation, to have inner peace and harmony disrupted

Core Motivation: to create harmony in the environment, to avoid conflicts and tension, to preserve things as they are, to resist whatever would be upsetting or disturbing to inner peace

Passion/The Personal Challenge: Sloth—a deep state of denial and avoidance of all things: feelings, reality, challenges, hope, presence, humanity

Fixation/The Trap: Indolence—avoidance of external influences that may force an awakening to the pain, suffering, or anything that may be disturbing

Virtue/The Gift: Action—find the presence to recognize own strength and power and then take right action to bring peace and harmony to not only self but to everyone

Wings: Eight and One

Arrows: Three and Six

Nines want to be:

- able to find unity and wholeness

- resistant to change

- able to find harmony and peace for others

- comfortable and at ease

- able to emphasize the positive

- away from conflict or tension

Nines do not want to be:

- in conflict with loved ones

- cut off or separated from others

- angry, upset, or disturbed

- in a position to have habits or routines interrupted

- emotionally uncomfortable

- forced to face unpleasant realities

LEVELS OF DEVELOPMENT
AS A TYPE NINE

HEALTHY LEVELS OF DEVELOPMENT

As a Nine operating within the healthy Levels of Development, you become an engaged and forceful leader. You are willing to face conflict with an unexpectedly powerful impact and a calm but present serenity. You become a fierce defender of humanity, a quiet but surprisingly assertive leader on the front lines of the battle for love, compassion, and reconnection. You navigate life through inner strength and the courage to honor your authentic self in the face of divisiveness, confrontation, and conflict. The need for maintaining inner peace and stability at any cost evolves into an externalization of finding peace and harmony for everyone through honest, reasoned, and harmonious approaches. You can take the right action and remain present without the fear of being affected by disruptive influences. You recognize the power of your voice in the face of challenges and step into a leadership role with courage and intentional presence.

AVERAGE LEVELS OF DEVELOPMENT

Most humans reside within these average levels and fluctuate up or down depending on the circumstances they find themselves in. As you drop down into the average Levels of Development, the ego agenda begins to take over. The fluctuations can create opportunities for you to pause and cultivate the presence you need to examine your thoughts and actions and course correct. This allows for you to move back up in the levels and avoid falling back into unhealthy patterns of behavior and thought. However, as the ability for self-reflection and course correction wanes, you begin to project a false sense of calm, and you may fall into old patterns of "numbing out." You can become unwilling to engage authentically and begin to struggle with your ability to maintain your presence. You may become emotionally numb and self-effacing. You deflect authentic reflection, embracing a "going with the flow" mentality as you fall into apathy. The "not my problem" outlook becomes a fallback, leading you down a path of denying or justifying your complicity in the widespread disconnection of humanity. You may experience a flicker of hope when you begin to find presence, but it can be short-lived as you find the presence too disruptive to your routine of passivity. The anger and passivity can morph into a wake-up call to step into a healthy space or it can deteriorate into a toxic pattern of thoughts and behaviors. Presence becomes your main obstacle at this level. It takes a great deal of self-reflection and inner work to rise up through the levels and avoid dropping further.

Unhealthy Levels of Development

As you drop into the unhealthy levels, you can become deeply repressed, ineffectual, unquestioningly loyal, and painfully angry. You actively justify your actions and beliefs from the unhealthy energy of Nine. If you are an unhealthy Nine, you may be capable of embodying true apathy; becoming destructively cavalier, distant, unfeeling, or indifferent, you have a repressed anger lurking within a cold and detached exterior. Anger and denial are the primary motivators that distort your reality, resulting in a disdain for humans who may disrupt your inner peace or force you to wake up to or acknowledge your anger. As an asleep Nine, you may feel hopeless in the face of challenges and change and often revert to a level of complete numbness that allows your inner peace to remain falsely still. Unhealthy Nines can often be found among the masses of the unquestioning and complacent, unwittingly attaching themselves to anything that lets them release their anger even if it is misdirected or unrelated. If you fall into the unhealthy levels of Nine, you can become so detached from humanity that you develop a complete disregard for basic human decency. Presence is a true challenge; when you neglect the importance of your inner voice and bury your true emotions, you remain too stubborn to wake up and deal with reality.

You can refer back to the Levels of Development to see where you are at any point in time. Make notes on your progress below:

_____

_____

_____

_____

_____

_____

WINGS

Remember, you have access to both wings. Some people identify strongly with one wing energy over the other, but both wings still affect how your dominant type appears.

NINE WITH A STRONG EIGHT WING

Willingness to fight for truth and justice and find solutions with strength and perseverance, assertive and alert, inability to control anger, rebellious and confrontational, aggressive and overly angry when provoked

NINE WITH A STRONG ONE WING

Principled in finding harmony, balanced perspective and a strong focus on helping improve the lives of others, highly principled in maintaining rigidity, passive-aggressive and self-righteous

ARROWS

Remember, you have access to both arrows, and you can move freely between these connections. This movement allows you to pick up positive and negative energies as needed and creates a warning system and a path for growth.

NINE'S ARROW TO THREE

Establish voice and presence with confidence, value, and charisma, actively seek out and maintain connections to others, easily overwhelmed and concerned about outside validation and judgment

NINE'S ARROW TO SIX

Energetic and alert, accountability and responsibility become driving motivators, reflective and focused, scattered and overwhelmed with fear and anxiety, indecisive, reactive, and insecure, outbursts of irrational anger

INSTINCTS

As balanced human beings, we naturally have all three instincts within us. However, we have a dominant instinct that we feel most comfortable with and a secondary instinct to support the dominant one. The third instinct is usually the least developed, therefore, an area that manifests as an unseen personal challenge.

SELF-PRESERVATION NINE

If you are a Self-Preservation Nine, you may be more easygoing and complacent, often finding comfort in the simplicity of life, and tend to be quieter and more reserved. Finding inner peace in your routines and ability to "zone out," you can lean into apathy as a means of coping with your anger and anxiety around not living up to your own expectations. You may have a hard time stepping out of your comfort zone to meet new people or create new experiences, but you are willing to go with the flow when you are surrounded by people you know or with whom you feel a level of comfort.

SOCIAL NINE

As a Social Nine, you may focus your energy outward on creating and assimilating into peaceful and harmonious groups. You tend to be more outgoing and flexible in your approach to connection and ability to find inner peace. In creating a clearly defined place within your group or family you often lose sight of what you really want or need and feel anxious or angry about your lack of personal development, similar to an unhealthy Two. You may have a tendency to merge your life with others, even in toxic environments, as long as you can find comfort and stability in the group.

SEXUAL NINE

As a Sexual Nine, you are more focused on creating strong bonds with others. You may use your energy to fuse with another person, often merging with the other person's emotions, beliefs, desires, and so on, which feels similar to the energy of Two. You probably have a more defined relationship with your anger as it is easily recognizable and expressed when your connections are jeopardized. Unlike the other instincts within the Nine, you might not have a problem with understanding and expressing your emotions. However, you typically find it difficult to define who you are outside of the person or persons with whom you have attached yourself.

NINE'S RESPONSES TO CONFLICTS

UNHEALTHY REACTION

Passive-aggressive behaviors, avoidance, denial, repression, "numbing out," self-effacing attitude, deflection, extreme dissociation, volcanic outburst of repressed/misplaced anger, a complete disregard for basic human decency when faced with difficult situations that may force you to wake up to your own anger and pain, acceptance of a delusional approach to life; in order to protect yourself from being disrupted or forced to wake up, you run away from challenges, oftentimes seeking out painless solutions to detach from being held accountable for your actions, which leads to a sense of fatigue when you become overwhelmed or disheartened by the current state of things

HEALTHY REACTION

Pausing for reflection and finding the strength of your presence, action, forcefulness, engagement, passion, supportive with purpose, open and receptive to ideas while maintaining universal truths, strong drive for peace and harmony bolstered by right action, kindhearted approaches, genuinely caring, down to earth, easygoing mentality, and generally calm, persistent, loyal, dedicated to the cause

Reflections on your experience of unhealthy and healthy responses:

_____

_____

_____

_____

_____

_____

_____

EXAMPLES OF NINE ENERGY

Barack Obama, Alicia Keys, Ronald Reagan, Colin Powell, Carl Jung, Abraham Lincoln, Gloria Steinem, Queen Elizabeth II, Joseph Campbell, Morgan Freeman, Dwight D. Eisenhower, Audrey Hepburn, Norman Rockwell, Gerald Ford, Walter Cronkite, Carl Rogers, Walt Disney, Ron Howard, Gary Cooper, Jimmy Stewart, James Taylor

Explore your connection to one or more of these people who demonstrate strong Nine energy. What is it about their character or personality that reminds you most of yourself?

_____

_____

_____

_____

_____

_____

_____

_____

_____

_____

_____

_____

_____

_____

_____

_____

How do you experience the different elements of Nine energy within yourself?

_____

_____

_____

_____

_____

_____

_____

_____

_____

_____

_____

_____

_____

_____

_____

_____

_____

_____

_____

_____

_____

What is your experience like with other
people who exhibit Nine energy?

_____

_____

_____

_____

_____

_____

_____

_____

_____

_____

_____

_____

_____

_____

_____

_____

_____

_____

_____

_____

_____

_____

Reflections on
BEING AN
ENNEAGRAM NINE

As you embark on this profound inner journey, it's essential to take a moment to revisit the very origin of your path. Within this section, we invite you to reflect upon the beginnings of your Enneagram journey and how it gently unfolded before you. Delving into past feelings and behaviors is a natural and important aspect of this process.

As a Nine, your remarkable strengths lie in your consistent ability to find peace and harmony in all things. The prompts provided here offer you a special opportunity for profound introspection.

It's quite likely that you had specific reactions when you first discovered your dominant energy at Type Nine. These reactions are all part of the ongoing journey as you transition from mere reactions to intentional responses. It's essential to explore your feelings but not to become ensnared or overwhelmed by what you feel. Remember, feelings are transient by nature. As you navigate through your emotions, you'll discover immense fulfillment at the deeper layers of this exploration. Embrace your innate curiosity and approach this journey with the wonder of a beginner's mind as you unveil more and more about your authentic self and how you present yourself to the world. In connecting with the reality of your inner guidance and greatness, you may be pleasantly surprised by the fears that once held you back.

It's important to note that not every attribute, characteristic, or behavior described at Type Nine will necessarily resonate with your unique energy experience. This is an incredible opportunity to unearth aspects of your being that have, until now, remained hidden from your conscious awareness. This profound self-discovery journey will open your mind, mend your heart, and rejuvenate your body in ways you may have never imagined. As you dive deep into this exploration, your spirit will gracefully embrace and embody your core values, aligning with your natural gift of peace and harmony. We wholeheartedly encourage you not to hold back, but to embrace this journey as it carries you to uncharted territories within your own being, revealing facets of yourself you have yet to explore. This is our heartfelt wish for you.

Grounding Meditation

As I move into self-reflection and internal exploration,
I will meditate on these prompts and gently notice
what comes up as I breathe into stillness.

I am ready to begin with three cleansing breaths.

I am releasing any tension that I am holding
in my body with each exhale.

I am grounded and present to the sensations in my body.

I am open and aware of the feelings in my heart.

I am not attached to the thoughts that float by.

I am ready to explore what being a Nine means to me.

I will embrace all aspects of my personality and gently
work toward becoming more accepting of myself.

My reactions when I discovered my dominant energy as a Type Nine:

_____
_____
_____
_____
_____
_____
_____
_____
_____
_____
_____
_____
_____
_____
_____
_____
_____
_____
_____
_____
_____
_____

My feelings about being a Nine:

_____

_____

_____

_____

_____

_____

_____

_____

_____

_____

_____

_____

_____

_____

_____

_____

_____

_____

_____

_____

_____

_____

_____

My hopes for discovering more about my Nine energy:

_____
_____
_____
_____
_____
_____
_____
_____
_____
_____
_____
_____
_____
_____
_____
_____
_____
_____
_____
_____
_____
_____

My fears around seeing myself as I truly am:

_____

_____

_____

_____

_____

_____

_____

_____

_____

_____

_____

_____

_____

_____

_____

_____

_____

_____

_____

_____

_____

_____

_____

Observations about myself that support Nine as my dominant type:

Aspects and descriptors of Nine energy that I do not feel connected with:

_____

_____

_____

_____

_____

_____

_____

_____

_____

_____

Are these aspects I do not feel connected with indicators
of any personal challenges that I may overlook?

_____

_____

_____

_____

_____

_____

_____

_____

What are my core values that align with my Nine energy?

_____

_____

_____

_____

_____

_____

_____

_____

_____

_____

_____

_____

_____

_____

_____

_____

_____

_____

_____

_____

_____

_____

Reflections on my actions and beliefs around my core values:

Ways I have honored my core values recently:

_____
_____
_____
_____
_____
_____
_____
_____
_____
_____
_____
_____
_____
_____
_____
_____
_____
_____
_____
_____
_____
_____

What do I wish people knew about me?

_____

_____

_____

_____

_____

_____

_____

_____

_____

_____

_____

_____

_____

_____

_____

_____

_____

_____

_____

_____

MY EARLY MESSAGES AND EXPERIENCES

As you embark on this journey, take a moment to reflect on the early messages and messengers that have shaped your path. You might discover that your childhood experiences with the distinctly peaceful energy emanating from Nine created a strong sense of discomfort with conflict and a desire to fade into the background in order to maintain your inner peace.

These initial reactions and responses, etched deep within you, were not merely fleeting notions but lasting imprints. You absorbed messages you may not have been consciously aware of, and they didn't simply pass through; instead, they were deeply ingrained in your very being. Retrieving them intentionally requires the assistance of a profound inner exploration. As you transitioned into adulthood, these feelings became an integral part of your approach to life. You may have developed an internal narrative that encouraged you to suppress your feelings and thoughts and dissociate from conflict and change. This approach served as a shield, guarding you from external influences, and allowed you to build a protective cocoon around your inner peace. In retrospect, this journey may reveal moments and connections deeply resonating with the energy of Type Nine.

As a Nine, resist the allure of passivity as you embark on this exploration. There might be that familiar pull toward indifference when you start this journey and begin to reawaken from within, but it's essential to remain present and welcome whatever unfolds for you. While the path from Type Nine to the more contemplative and present energies of the Enneagram can be challenging, it's a journey that holds a direct connection to joy, vitality, and love.

By diving deeper and reflecting on both the positive and challenging aspects of your childhood, you can unlock a wellspring of joy and aliveness that may have been buried over the years. Recall the simple joys of your youth; those moments that lit up your heart. These cherished memories serve as a direct pathway to rekindling the joy and fulfillment in this current chapter of your life. Taking the time to rediscover these childhood memories can be a beautiful way to reconnect with your authentic self and bring a sense of fulfillment and vibrancy into your life. It's a journey of self-discovery, a gentle reminder of the unique and remarkable individual that you've always been. So, open your heart to the wisdom of your inner child and let the light of joy, aliveness, and love shine through to help you remember who you are.

Grounding Meditation

As I move into self-reflection and internal exploration,
I will meditate on these prompts and gently notice
what comes up as I breathe into stillness.

I am ready to begin with three cleansing breaths.

I am inhaling peace and exhaling tension.

I am ready to embark on a journey into my past.

I will honor my experience as I recall childhood memories.

My past does not define me.

I can explore what was, accept what is, and embrace what will be.

My most vivid memory of how my Nine energy
showed up when I was a child:

_____
_____
_____
_____
_____
_____
_____
_____
_____
_____
_____
_____
_____
_____
_____
_____
_____
_____
_____
_____
_____
_____
_____

What are my feelings and reactions when others bring up
shared childhood memories that I do not remember?

_____

_____

_____

_____

_____

_____

_____

_____

_____

_____

_____

_____

_____

_____

_____

_____

_____

_____

_____

People and experiences that have brought me the most joy and peace:

I can create space in my life for more of these positive influences by:

_____

_____

_____

_____

_____

_____

_____

_____

_____

_____

_____

_____

_____

_____

_____

_____

_____

_____

_____

_____

_____

_____

What dreams for my future did I have as a child?

_____
_____
_____
_____
_____
_____
_____
_____
_____
_____
_____
_____
_____
_____
_____
_____
_____
_____
_____
_____
_____
_____
_____

Activities I enjoyed as a child:

_____
_____
_____
_____
_____
_____
_____
_____
_____
_____

Reflections on how these activities brought
feelings of pure joy and happiness:

_____
_____
_____
_____
_____
_____
_____
_____
_____
_____
_____
_____
_____

Happiness is part
of the flow of life.

If you remain rigid,
then happiness will
flow right past you.

Allow yourself
the gift of letting
go and ease into the
flow of whatever may
come your way.

I can cultivate small moments of happiness in my everyday life by:

Reflections on
MY PURPOSE AND
MY "PUZZLE PIECE"

Let's imagine the world as a puzzle, and envision each one of us holding a piece that, when placed, helps create a more complete and harmonious world. You possess a truly unique gift to offer to the world; imagine it as if you are the holder of a vital piece of a grand, intricate puzzle. Yet to truly offer this gift, we must be willing to embark on our own inner journey.

When we embrace this inner work, we gain the strength and clarity needed to step forward and make our unique contribution. This courageous act sets a beautiful chain reaction in motion, allowing others to find the inspiration and courage to contribute as well.

In the upcoming section, we extend a warm invitation to you, encouraging you to (re)awaken the passions and interests that stir deep within your soul, those beautiful aspects of yourself that you'd love to revive and share with the world. You might notice a strong emotional response to social injustices; this very reaction could be a hidden passion or a point of personal growth waiting to be unveiled. Your dedication to a particular societal issue could hold the key to discovering your unique place and voice in contributing to the collective healing of humanity. Perhaps your heart resonates deeply with environmental causes, or you're deeply affected by the suffering of animals. This is your precious opportunity to unearth and delve into what truly matters to you.

Consider what consistently draws your attention and captivates your mind—whether it's art, music, literature, social causes, theater, science, spirituality, parenting, or family. Why do these topics continue to surface for you? Use this opportunity to delve deeper into the aspects of your life where you find an abundance of energy or even areas that may initially appear exhausting. This is your chance to sculpt and refine your unique puzzle piece (and yes, we all have one or more) so that you can stand with gratitude and presence, fully aware of the significance of your contribution. As we awaken to our own purpose, we naturally have the capacity to awaken those around us, igniting a chain reaction of positive change.

Explore the boundless possibilities that lie ahead, and remember that your piece of the puzzle is invaluable to creating a world that's more complete, compassionate, and connected.

Grounding Meditation

As I move into self-reflection and internal exploration,
I will meditate on these prompts and gently notice
what comes up as I breathe into stillness.

I am ready to begin with three cleansing breaths.

I am releasing any tension that I am holding
in my body with each exhale.

I am inhaling into the wholeness of the Universe
and exhaling whatever may be troubling me.

I am open to exploring my place in the world.

I am willing to explore my purpose and (re)discover the
unique puzzle piece I hold to contribute to the world.

My life has meaning, and my presence matters.

I am accepting of whatever comes up for me at this moment.

What contributions do I want to make in this world?

Reflections on how I align my daily actions with my
deeper sense of establishing peace and harmony:

_____

_____

_____

_____

_____

_____

_____

_____

_____

_____

_____

_____

_____

_____

_____

_____

_____

_____

_____

_____

_____

What inspires me?

How have I limited myself in finding sources of inspiration? How can I open myself to new experiences? Have I considered engaging with new people, places, music, art, literature, and so on?

What comes up for me when I think about the activities, relationships, and causes that I am drawn to?

_____

_____

_____

_____

_____

_____

_____

_____

_____

_____

_____

_____

_____

_____

_____

_____

_____

_____

_____

_____

_____

_____

How do I avoid applying myself, taking action, or getting involved
with things where my presence could make a big difference?

_____

_____

_____

_____

_____

_____

_____

_____

_____

_____

_____

_____

_____

_____

_____

_____

_____

_____

_____

_____

_____

The quality
of your life
will reflect
how deep you
are willing
to go to touch
your own soul.

What personal, professional, spiritual, and/or life
roles contribute to my sense of identity?

_____

_____

_____

_____

_____

_____

_____

_____

_____

_____

_____

_____

_____

_____

_____

_____

_____

_____

_____

_____

_____

I am very passionate about:

What do I wish I could do to make the world around me better?

_____

_____

_____

_____

_____

_____

_____

_____

_____

_____

_____

_____

_____

_____

_____

_____

_____

_____

_____

_____

_____

_____

Reflections on my current projects, work, and/or endeavors:

How are these feeding my spirit or draining my energy?

_____

_____

_____

_____

_____

_____

_____

_____

_____

_____

_____

_____

_____

_____

_____

_____

_____

_____

_____

_____

_____

_____

Reflections on
HOW MY NINE ENERGY SHOWS UP

As a Nine, the central principle of harmony imbues your every experience. Within the average Levels of Development, as you are basking in the tranquility and peace of your inner world, you might find yourself feeling justified in your actions, at ease with your behaviors, all while gently harboring an underlying fear of conflict.

Those who resonate with Type Nine embody a deep and resounding desire to live in a state of peace and harmony. This desire tends to manifest most profoundly when conflict, change, and chaos are the defining elements of any given situation. However, when you unintentionally relinquish your innate ability to mediate for peace and slide into the default state of detachment and withdrawal, your yearning for finding harmony and peace can become distorted, giving way to a pattern of self-forgetting. This is precisely where the transformative inner work plays a crucial role, helping you raise the vibration of your energy to a healthier level.

As you release the hold that conflict has on your energy and rediscover your agency to mediate and foster peace, you find alignment with a profound spirit. Love, peace, harmony, and your authentic capacity to honor and connect with all of humanity illuminate the path to rediscovering who you are at your core. You become open to engaging with the complexities and challenges of the world, ultimately embracing the flowing tapestry of life as an extraordinary gift. In this often tumultuous world where peace may be elusive, your presence shines brightly and is openly received by those around you. The effect you have on the world is not only valued but warmly welcomed and very much needed.

Your journey toward embracing your role as a mediator and guardian of harmony is an invitation to discover the authentic self that you may have hidden away as self-forgetting has taken over. It's a path that encourages you to actively engage with the world's messiness while holding the torch of peace and love. As you tread this path, remember to remain openhearted, as it is through your warm and inviting presence that you bring solace and harmony to the world around you. Your capacity to embrace harmony and spread peace is a gift that enriches not only your life but the lives of those fortunate enough to know you.

Grounding Meditation

As I move into self-reflection and internal exploration,
I will meditate on these prompts and gently notice
what comes up as I breathe into stillness.

I am ready to begin with three cleansing breaths.

I am releasing any tension that I am holding
in my body with each exhale.

I am inhaling into presence and exhaling negativity and judgment.

I am ready to explore my Nineness.

I will allow myself to reflect on how I show up to myself and others.

I will acknowledge any judgment or criticism that
arises with Grace and compassion for myself.

I will embrace all parts of my being as valid and valuable.

I will release the need to ignore my own needs, wants,
and desires and explore what I really care about.

Reflect back on the "Levels of Development" section (page 14) for this exercise.

I was aware of the high side of my Nine energy this week when:

_____

_____

_____

_____

_____

_____

_____

_____

_____

_____

_____

_____

_____

_____

_____

_____

_____

_____

Reflect back on the "Levels of Development" section (page 14) for this exercise.

I was aware of the low side of my Nine energy this week when:

_____

_____

_____

_____

_____

_____

_____

_____

_____

_____

_____

_____

_____

_____

_____

_____

_____

_____

_____

_____

Harmony requires patience, practice, and authenticity.

My reflections on what harmony means to me:

_____
_____
_____
_____
_____
_____
_____
_____
_____
_____
_____
_____
_____
_____
_____
_____
_____
_____
_____
_____
_____
_____
_____
_____

My reactions to the disruption of my inner peace:

_____

_____

_____

_____

_____

_____

_____

_____

_____

_____

_____

_____

_____

_____

_____

_____

_____

_____

_____

_____

_____

_____

Ways that I experience challenges to "waking up":

_____

_____

_____

_____

_____

_____

_____

_____

_____

_____

_____

_____

_____

_____

_____

_____

_____

_____

_____

_____

_____

_____

_____

_____

How am I complacent? What does it look like,
and how does it make me feel?

_____

_____

_____

_____

_____

_____

_____

_____

_____

_____

_____

_____

_____

_____

_____

_____

_____

_____

_____

_____

_____

_____

What parts of myself do I hide from others and why?

_____
_____
_____
_____
_____
_____
_____
_____
_____
_____
_____
_____
_____
_____
_____
_____
_____
_____
_____
_____
_____
_____
_____
_____

What do other people do for me that makes me feel seen?

_____

_____

_____

_____

_____

_____

_____

_____

_____

_____

_____

_____

_____

_____

_____

_____

_____

_____

_____

How do I make others feel seen?

_____
_____
_____
_____
_____
_____
_____
_____
_____
_____
_____
_____
_____
_____
_____
_____
_____
_____
_____
_____
_____
_____
_____
_____
_____
_____

You must embrace your own being and accept yourself exactly as you are. This is a first step in belonging. Never let anyone determine whether or not you belong.

That choice is yours.

What does belonging mean to me? How have I sought
out belonging and connection in my life?

_____

_____

_____

_____

_____

_____

_____

_____

_____

_____

_____

_____

_____

_____

_____

_____

_____

_____

_____

_____

How do other people describe me?

Fill the page with words, phrases, and drawings.
Allow for the flow of creativity and freedom.

How do I describe myself?

Fill the page with words, phrases, and drawings.
Allow for the flow of creativity and freedom.

PRESENCE

As a Nine, one of the most enriching journeys you can embark upon is the one that leads you to your authentic self, where true peace, love, and inner harmony thrive. On this path, you'll find that one of the most significant challenges you face is the daily repression of your true self, all in the effort to maintain an environment untouched by the turbulence of life. This may involve navigating through passive-aggressive behaviors, uttering yes when your heart screams no, avoiding conflict to uphold superficial connections, and even drifting into a slumber state of denial instead of addressing the realities of existence.

Amid the gentle waters of your inner world, the obstacle of presence often looms large. It beckons you to fully embrace your genuine emotions and beliefs while recognizing the profound impact you wield upon the world around you. Your ability to maintain this sense of presence is intrinsically linked to the concept of self-forgetting. Over the years, the act of repressing your true self might have led to a forgetfulness of your own desires and dreams. What is it that truly brings you joy? What are your hopes and aspirations? What do you envision for your life's journey? These questions can indeed stir complex emotions, particularly for those who resonate with Type Nine.

Whether consciously or unconsciously, a self-forgetting mentality might have taken root, and the awakening to the realities of life can stir strong emotions within. As a Nine, you maintain a meticulous control over what enters your inner space, both physically and emotionally, to preserve your sense of tranquility. This can perpetuate your primary defense mechanism of narcotization as a Nine. Delving into the ways you've numbed yourself and the sources that have encouraged this behavior can be an enlightening and healing process. Through this journey, remember to remain awake and aware of yourself, and grant yourself the compassion to reclaim your right to stand in your own truth. Recognize the profound value of your voice and its impact on the world, for your presence matters.

In this transformative process of self-discovery and awakening, consider this a voyage into the heart of who you truly are. By embarking on this journey with an open heart, you can rediscover your authentic self, reconnect with your hopes and dreams, and fully embrace the joy and happiness that life has to offer. With each step you take, you invite the richness of authenticity and presence into your world, forging a path to a more fulfilling and vibrant existence.

Grounding Meditation

As I move into self-reflection and internal exploration,
I will meditate on these prompts and gently notice
what comes up as I breathe into stillness.

I am ready to begin with three cleansing breaths.

I am inhaling peace and love and exhaling judgment and criticism.

I am present. I am grounded and awakened with every breath.

My presence matters.

I will access Grace and loving kindness as I honor what surfaces.

I will remain in presence and choose a path
of empathy and compassion.

What does it look like when I am fully present?

_____

_____

_____

_____

_____

_____

_____

_____

_____

_____

_____

_____

_____

_____

_____

_____

_____

_____

_____

_____

_____

_____

What does it look like when I "numb out"?

_____
_____
_____
_____
_____
_____
_____
_____
_____
_____
_____
_____
_____
_____
_____
_____
_____
_____
_____
_____
_____
_____
_____
_____

What causes me to shut down and fall asleep to what is happening around me? How can I explore this deeper without feeling the need to shut down further?

_____

_____

_____

_____

_____

_____

_____

_____

_____

_____

_____

_____

_____

_____

_____

_____

_____

_____

_____

_____

What situations, people, emotions, and
responsibilities do I tend to avoid and why?

_____

_____

_____

_____

_____

_____

_____

_____

_____

_____

_____

_____

_____

_____

_____

_____

_____

_____

_____

_____

_____

_____

What parts of myself have I forgotten over the years?

What do I care about?

What makes me feel energized and engaged?

_____

_____

_____

_____

_____

_____

_____

_____

_____

_____

_____

_____

_____

_____

_____

_____

_____

_____

_____

_____

_____

_____

What steps can I take to pause and change my course of
action when I notice I have started losing presence?

_____

_____

_____

_____

_____

_____

_____

_____

_____

_____

_____

_____

_____

_____

_____

_____

_____

_____

_____

_____

_____

_____

_____

_____

What are my unique talents, gifts, and skills that I can offer to the world?

What truly makes me who I am?

We are surrounded
by Grace in every
moment of our lives.
Grace always comes
through when we allow
ourselves to embrace
and experience the
warmth of its existence.
Let love and light in.

Allow Grace to
lead your actions today.

What does Grace look like for me as a Nine?

MY RELATIONSHIP TO ANGER

Anger can sometimes feel like an unnatural and unwelcome emotion for individuals who resonate with Type Nine, since they are often known for their peaceful and harmonious disposition. During moments of pain and suffering, whether originating internally or externally, you may experience a visceral response that manifests as bodily reactions, instinctual internal or external rage, and a strong desire to regain a sense of control over your surroundings—sometimes this manifests as removing yourself from whatever may be affecting your inner peace.

As a Nine, you might find yourself facing a formidable wall of anger and rage surrounding an unhealed or unexplored internal wound. This metaphorical wall can act as a barrier, concealing your authentic self, and how you choose to address or ignore it is a deeply personal journey. This internal turmoil often stems from early memories of rejection, betrayal, neglect, feeling unimportant, or struggling with feelings of inadequacy. Each person approaches this barrier uniquely, and when we find ourselves ensnared in a toxic behavioral pattern, this internal anger can often manifest as outward expressions directed at others. The journey of inner work entails the exploration of strategies to embrace, articulate, and ultimately transform this powerful emotion.

Anger and forgiveness, intertwined companions in the human experience, form a complex concept often misunderstood. Beyond benefiting others, forgiveness frees you from emotional burdens, opening the path to love and happiness. It enables your authentic expression of love, aligning with your creation. Great ascended masters stress the importance of forgiveness, providing invaluable lessons we sometimes forget. Remember, forgiveness is integral to self-love, allowing your authentic self to return to innocence and purity by freeing yourself from pain. It's the ultimate act of self-respect, empowering and embracing your inner strength.

In this section, you'll have the chance to reflect on and explore your relationship with anger. Approach the journey with patience and self-compassion. These exercises are designed to guide you toward reconnecting with the abundance of goodness, love, and light that reside within you.

Grounding Meditation

As I move into self-reflection and internal exploration,
I will meditate on these prompts and gently notice
what comes up as I breathe into stillness.

I am ready to begin with three cleansing breaths.

I am inhaling a sense of calm and peace and
exhaling tension and anxiety.

I acknowledge my anger and am willing to
gently explore what's underneath.

I will explore my relationship to my anger
with patience and understanding.

I accept anger as a natural human emotion.

My anger does not define who I am.

I will accept my anger as an internal warning system to
seek out opportunities for growth and self-reflection.

What/who makes me angry?

How do I express my anger? What does it look like?

_____
_____
_____
_____
_____
_____
_____
_____
_____
_____
_____
_____
_____
_____
_____
_____
_____
_____
_____
_____
_____
_____
_____

I notice I tend to repress my angry Nine energy when:

_____

_____

_____

_____

_____

_____

_____

_____

_____

_____

_____

_____

_____

_____

_____

_____

_____

_____

_____

_____

What does it look like when I become passive-aggressive?

What does it look like when my anger causes me to detach from others?

What/who helps me when I feel the anger rising inside me?

_____

_____

_____

_____

_____

_____

_____

_____

_____

_____

_____

_____

_____

_____

_____

_____

_____

_____

_____

_____

_____

_____

What/who do I need to forgive?

_____
_____
_____
_____
_____
_____
_____
_____
_____
_____
_____
_____
_____
_____
_____
_____
_____
_____
_____

Forgiveness doesn't excuse their behavior.
Forgiveness prevents their behavior
from destroying your heart.

UNKNOWN

Do I know how to forgive? What is holding me back from accessing forgiveness for myself and others?

What stresses me out and what are my reactions?

What are a few ways I can release my stress?

_____

_____

_____

_____

_____

_____

_____

_____

_____

_____

_____

_____

_____

_____

_____

_____

_____

_____

_____

_____

_____

_____

_____

Reflections on
MY VIRTUE OF ACTION

The virtue for Type Nine is action. This virtue truly comes to life when you view it as a fluid energy, one that empowers you to traverse life with a profound sense of purpose, all while staying firmly rooted in the present, unshaken by the disruptions that may come your way. This unique gift can be aptly characterized as "right action"—an innate talent to discern what requires your attention and precisely how to undertake it. It all emanates from a wellspring of inner strength and unwavering presence. As a Nine, this virtue of right action becomes attainable when you wholeheartedly commit to the inner work and tap into the high side of Nine.

Throughout your journey toward this virtue, you may encounter familiar roadblocks, with the trap of indolence being a particularly daunting challenge. The fear of dealing with conflict and the risk of losing your inner peace and harmony to external forces can lead to a tendency to retreat inward and withdraw. This is precisely where the inner work process becomes paramount. By working through these barriers, you become confident in your ability to stand your ground, staying present amid life's challenges while maintaining your inner serenity. You find the courage to confront conflicts with an unexpectedly powerful impact, radiating a calm yet unwavering presence.

Your invitation to step into a transformative space welcomes you with open arms, encouraging you to embrace your role as a dedicated advocate for humanity, a gentle yet remarkably influential leader at the forefront of the battle for love, compassion, and reconnection. You gracefully navigate life, drawing from your inner well of strength to embrace your authentic self, even when faced with divisiveness, confrontation, and conflict. What initially drove you to seek inner peace and stability at all costs has now evolved into a noble mission to nurture peace and harmony for all, employing sincere, rational, and harmonious approaches. This is where you wholeheartedly manifest your virtue of right action. You've come to understand the incredible power of your voice in the face of challenges and, with unwavering courage and presence, have embraced a pivotal role that radiates warmth and invites others to join in the journey toward love and light.

Exploring your connection and path to the virtue of action is another step toward unearthing your true, authentic self. Embrace this journey with an open heart, for it is an invitation to express your inner strength and light in the face of life's complexities. Step into the person you were created to be, because your presence matters in this world.

Grounding Meditation

As I move into self-reflection and internal exploration,
I will meditate on each of these prompts and gently notice
what comes up for me as I breathe into stillness.

I am ready to begin with three cleansing breaths.

I am inhaling into presence and exhaling any
reluctance or anger I may be holding on to.

As I explore the virtue of action, I seek
opportunities to allow it to flow naturally.

Right action is my access to Grace.

Right action is always present within me.

I allow myself to embrace the gift of right action
by releasing what no longer serves me.

How has right action manifested in my life, and what did it bring?

How has right action eluded me? What comes
up for me by asking this question?

_____

_____

_____

_____

_____

_____

_____

_____

_____

_____

_____

_____

_____

_____

_____

_____

_____

_____

_____

Action
transforms
intention into
engagement
and dreams
into reality.

What am I willing to surrender to embrace right action?

_____

_____

_____

_____

_____

_____

_____

_____

_____

_____

_____

_____

_____

_____

_____

_____

_____

_____

_____

_____

_____

When do I notice my tendency toward indolence and self-forgetting fading and my ability to access the virtue of right action developing?

Reflecting on my challenges with presence and my relationship to anger, can I explore my path to the embodiment of right action?

What do I need to take responsibility for in my life?

What small actions can I take right now to bring myself
into the present moment, such as taking a deep breath,
stretching, running, or savoring a sip of tea or coffee?

_____

_____

_____

_____

_____

_____

_____

_____

What are a few mantras I will use daily to bring myself back to the present
and move into a space where I can access the virtue of right action?

Example: I will find presence in everything I do and
remain engaged with clarity and perseverance.

_____

_____

_____

_____

_____

_____

_____

Discovering Connections to
OTHER ENNEAGRAM ENERGIES

Consider the Enneagram energies as nine individual gifts, each uniquely enriching the tapestry of your being. Within each of us, these nine energies coexist, and far too often, our fixation on our Enneagram type limits our perspective, hindering exploration of the eight other invaluable energies residing within us. It's vital to recognize that every human being requires the presence of these nine energies to achieve wholeness and completeness.

At each point of the Enneagram, a precious gift awaits, illuminating the path of self-discovery. At point One the gift is integrity, a beacon that guides you with a resolute moral compass. Point Two bestows the gift of pure love, fostering a spirit of generosity and an open heart for giving and receiving. Point Three endows you with the drive to accomplish and achieve great things, not just for personal gain but for the greater good of all. Point Four graces you with the capacity to embrace the world's beauty, holding it through love, empathy, and profound compassion while connecting deeply with human emotions. Point Five gifts you with the power of observation and the ability to discern solutions that might otherwise go unnoticed. At point Six you receive the gift of resilience, enabling you to cultivate the awareness of what is needed to keep us all protected, prepared, and unwavering in the face of adversity. Point Seven brings the gift of optimism, positivity, and spontaneity, infusing even the most challenging tasks with the spirit of joyfulness. Point Eight's gift is leadership, guiding us forward with the purity and strength of an innocent heart, always mindful of keeping our collective well-being intact. Finally, at point Nine, you are blessed with the gift of pure peace, a peace that transcends understanding and can only arise from a heart transformed by light and love.

Imagine that someone has lovingly gifted you with these nine beautifully wrapped presents. Why would you choose to open only one?

In this section, you are encouraged to embark on a journey through all nine Enneagram energies, to explore the connections to your wings, lines, and arrows, as well as the points that may not be part of your primary access. It's important to remember that you always have access to all nine energies, and sometimes, it takes a more deliberate effort to unearth these connections. Embrace this exploration with an open heart, for it's a step toward a deeper understanding of your authentic, multifaceted self, filled with infinite possibilities.

Grounding Meditation

As I move into self-reflection and internal exploration,
I will meditate on these prompts and gently notice
what comes up as I breathe into stillness.

I am ready to begin with three cleansing breaths.

I am inhaling into expansiveness and exhaling constriction.

I have the gift of all nine Enneagram energies within me.

I can freely explore my energy at all nine points.

I am not limited by my type.

I acknowledge my energy and connection to point Three and
point Six and utilize them for growth and awareness.

I can freely access my wings at point Eight and point One.

The Body Center: 8-9-1

In the Body Center, we gain access to our body's wisdom and gut intuition. The Body Center energy is focused on action—affecting the world or environment to avoid being influenced, controlled, or limited by it, and expressing anger or rage in different ways.

What does it look like for me to access
the energies within the Body Center?

Eight

_____

_____

_____

_____

_____

Nine

_____

_____

_____

_____

_____

One

_____

_____

_____

_____

_____

THE HEART CENTER: 2-3-4

In the Heart Center, we gain access to our capacity for emotional honesty and human connection. The Heart Center energy is focused on emotions, self-image, and value—determining your identity and the value you place on your identity plays a key role in how you access the Heart Center energy.

What does it look like for me to access the
energies within the Heart Center?

Two

_____

_____

_____

_____

_____

Three

_____

_____

_____

_____

_____

Four

_____

_____

_____

_____

_____

THE HEAD CENTER: 5-6-7

In the Head Center, we gain access to our ability to reflect, process, and internalize information. The wisdom we have access to in the Head Center energies allows us to cultivate the space we need for objectivity and inner guidance.

What does it look like for me to access the
energies within the Head Center?

Five

_____

_____

_____

_____

_____

Six

_____

_____

_____

_____

_____

Seven

_____

_____

_____

_____

_____

Do I face any challenges when connecting to particular
Enneagram energies? Can I explore this further?

_____

_____

_____

_____

_____

_____

_____

_____

_____

_____

_____

_____

_____

_____

_____

_____

_____

_____

_____

_____

_____

_____

Reflecting on the connection to my Eight wing, how can Eight energy bring me the grounded focus and forceful abundance of energy I need to remain present and engaged?

_____

_____

_____

_____

_____

_____

_____

_____

_____

_____

_____

_____

_____

_____

_____

_____

_____

_____

_____

You find peace not by rearranging the circumstances of your life, but by realizing who you are at the deepest level.

ECKHART TOLLE

Reflecting on the connection to my One wing, how can
One energy bring me clarity and principled focus, and
strengthen my ability to follow through with things?

_____

_____

_____

_____

_____

_____

_____

_____

_____

_____

_____

_____

_____

_____

_____

_____

_____

_____

_____

_____

_____

_____

When the winds of change blow, some people build walls and others build windmills.

CHINESE PROVERB

At point Nine, I share a connection to point Three, which provides an opportunity to explore the gifts and challenges of this energy. On the upside, this energy can help me establish my voice and presence with confidence and assertiveness, and help me actively seek out connections. On the downside, this energy can make me feel overwhelmed and create narcissistic tendencies. How have I experienced Three energy in my life?

_____

_____

_____

_____

_____

_____

_____

_____

_____

_____

_____

_____

_____

_____

_____

_____

_____

_____

_____

_____

If your compassion does not include yourself, it is incomplete.

CHUANG TZU

What does it look like when I tap into the abundance of charisma, inner motivation, and presence at point Three? How does my connection to point Three affect my actions, behaviors, and beliefs?

_____

_____

_____

_____

_____

_____

_____

_____

_____

_____

_____

_____

_____

_____

_____

_____

_____

_____

_____

_____

_____

_____

The great science of living happily
is to live in the present.

PYTHAGORAS

At point Nine, I share a connection to point Six, which provides an opportunity to explore the gifts and challenges of this energy. On the upside, this energy can allow me to find perspective, stay alert, seek out solutions, and keep me focused on things I am responsible for. On the downside, this energy can make me feel scattered and overwhelmed and lead me to become reactive and angry. How have I experienced Six energy in my life?

_____

_____

_____

_____

_____

_____

_____

_____

_____

_____

_____

_____

_____

_____

_____

_____

_____

_____

_____

_____

When we tackle obstacles, we find hidden reserves of courage and resilience we did not know we had. And it is only when we are faced with failure do we realize that these resources were always there within us. We only need to find them and move on with our lives.

A. P. J. Abdul Kalam

What does it look like when I am able to channel the focus, accountability, and motivation to embrace my responsibilities at point Six? How does my connection to point Six affect my actions, behaviors, and beliefs?

We are formed and molded by our thoughts.
Those whose minds are shaped by selfless
thoughts give joy when they speak or act.

BUDDHA

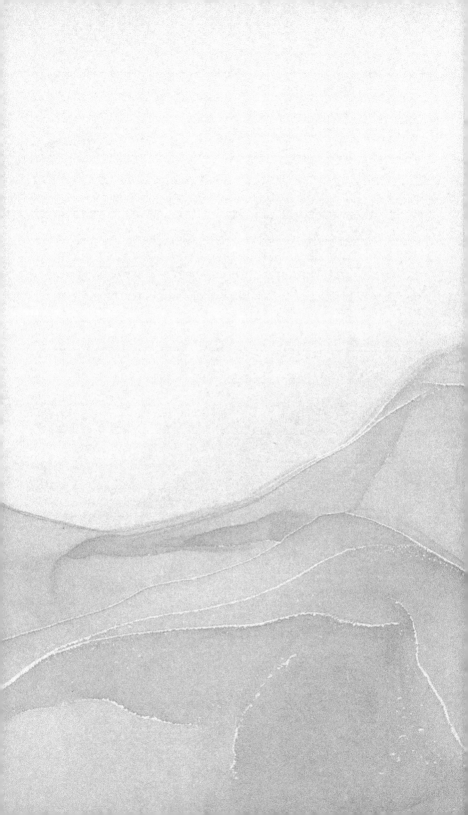

Resources for

CONTINUED EXPLORATION

If you would like to continue your Enneagram journey,
we invite you to visit our resources hub at:

DeborahEgerton.com/RESOURCES

and explore all of the resources we have gathered for you.
This resource hub is updated frequently, so make sure you
check back when you feel the need for a little inspiration.

You are also encouraged to read my books:

*Know Justice Know Peace: A Transformative Journey of Social Justice,
Anti-Racism, and Healing through the Power of the Enneagram*

*Enneagram Made Easy: Explore the Nine Personality Types of the
Enneagram to Open Your Heart, Find Joy, and Discover Your True Self*

**For easy access to the resources hub, use
your smartphone to scan this QR code:**

ABOUT THE AUTHOR

Deborah Threadgill Egerton, Ph.D., is an internationally respected psychotherapist, best-selling author, certified Enneagram teacher, unity and belonging advocate for the healing of humanity, consultant, coach, and spiritual teacher. Dr. Egerton specializes in working with the Enneagram to facilitate intentional change in individuals and organizations.

Affectionately referred to as "Dr. E," she has attained IEA Certification with Distinction for her groundbreaking utilization of the Enneagram in the realm of humanitarian healing. Her work is dedicated to dismantling marginalization and transcending the divisive practice of "othering," offering a guiding path toward the harmonious unification of our global community through the transformative forces of kindness and compassion. Dr. E serves as the president of the International Enneagram Association, the global entity responsible for educating, certifying, and accrediting practitioners, teachers, and schools. In her tenure with the IEA, she has been instrumental in fostering an environment of greater inclusivity and accessibility within the global Enneagram community. Her unwavering commitment to justice, equity, diversity, and inclusion has earned her the affectionate title of "Enneagram JEDI" among her peers.

Dr. E extends her coaching and mentoring expertise to a diverse spectrum of individuals, including best-selling authors, top-tier executives, spiritual luminaries, accomplished therapists, and a myriad of coaches, each hailing from distinct and varied backgrounds. For more than two decades, her work has focused on guiding humanity toward a deeper and more compassionate approach to inner work by harnessing the insights of the Enneagram. Her innovative approach to using the Enneagram in social justice and anti-racism work created a blueprint to reconnect people across all dimensions of diversity and has been implemented in various organizations and entities across the globe. She focuses her work on individuals and organizations to help them release false historical narratives and open their minds and hearts to a more compassionate and connected approach to life.

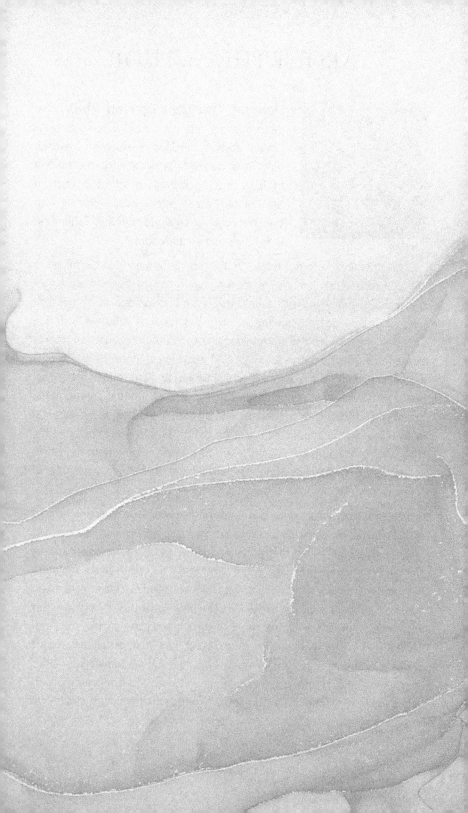

We hope you enjoyed this Hay House book. If you'd like to receive our online catalog featuring additional information on Hay House books and products, or if you'd like to find out more about the Hay Foundation, please contact:

Hay House LLC, P.O. Box 5100, Carlsbad, CA 92018-5100
(760) 431-7695 or (800) 654-5126
www.hayhouse.com® • www.hayfoundation.org

———

Published in Australia by:
Hay House Australia Publishing Pty Ltd
18/36 Ralph St., Alexandria NSW 2015
Phone: +61 (02) 9669 4299
www.hayhouse.com.au

Published in the United Kingdom by:
Hay House UK Ltd
The Sixth Floor, Watson House,
54 Baker Street, London W1U 7BU
Phone: +44 (0) 203 927 7290
www.hayhouse.co.uk

Published in India by:
Hay House Publishers (India) Pvt Ltd
Muskaan Complex, Plot No. 3,
B-2, Vasant Kunj, New Delhi 110 070
Phone: +91 11 41761620
www.hayhouse.co.in

———

Access New Knowledge.
Anytime. Anywhere.

Learn and evolve at your own pace
with the world's leading experts.

www.hayhouseU.com

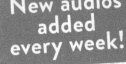